THE LAND IS A PAINTED THING

Also by Carrie Bennett

biography of water

THE LAND IS A PAINTED THING

Carrie Bennett

THE HILARY THAM CAPITAL COLLECTION
2016 Selections by Kimiko Hahn

THE WORD WORKS
WASHINGTON, D.C.

THE WORD WORKS
P.O. Box 42164
Washington, D.C. 20015
editor@wordworksbooks.org

Cover art and design: Cheri Jacobs
Author photograph: Jeremy Blackowicz

LCCN: 2015960104
ISBN: 978-1-944585-00-6

ACKNOWLEDGMENTS

My thanks to the editors of the following journals where many of these poems first appeared in earlier versions and some with different titles: *Boston Review, Caketrain, Denver Quarterly, The Destroyer, Field,* and *Kelsey Street Blog.* And to *Caketrain* and *The Destroyer* for nominating the poems they published for Pushcart Prizes.

I would like to thank Kimiko Hahn for selecting *The Land Is a Painted Thing,* Nancy White and Karren Alenier for their unwavering support, and Cole Swensen and Claudia Keelan for their generosity. Special thanks to Amaranth Borsuk, Jessica Bozek, Brigitte Byrd, Cheryl Clark Vermeulen, Nadia Herman Colburn, Kevin McLellan, Lilly McCrea, and Anna Ross for their keen poetic eyes and continued belief in this book. My grateful admiration to visual artists Kelvy Bird and Gee Wong whose artwork inspired and informed my conception of the land as a painted thing. And my gratitude to Cheri Jacobs for her beautiful cover art. My love and thanks to Jeremy for always sitting next to me while I worried over the world of this book. And finally, my love for the ornery and one-eyed tabby cat, Sammy, who acted as my dystopian muse and whose spirit still lives on in a great sky-field all her own.

CONTENTS

III.

IV.

"What are my eyes for if they can see but see nothing?"
—Jenny Erpenbeck, *The Book of Words*

"What will come has already come."
—William Kentridge, *The Refusal of Time*

I.

TRANSPLANT FACTORY

We filed into the room. We positioned ourselves along the white walls, our mouths were closed and waiting. The room was surrounded with shuffling feet and sighs. Someone covered her face with her hands. Near the ceiling rows of fluorescent bulbs shone starkly, loudspeakers hung in each corner.

Stand still, said a voice we had never heard. Someone coughed quietly, someone began to cry soundlessly.

You no longer know your own names, the voice told us. Watch how your bodies refuse submission. Time became a pile of snow. Static filled the room like cataracted stars. At that moment I looked out the window and the sky unburdened itself and forgot it ever knew light.

ENTERING THE MACHINE

It was now our job to bury our eyes deep in a drawer. Every night we washed the stained surfaces. We dreamed the same bridge, the same factory, the same opaque sky. To make us understand they told us our bodies were like the fields surrounding our new home. Our survival was in this belief.

PLEASE REMAIN SILENT

In anticipation of the daily meetings I scrubbed my eyes. Other samples were to be considered: skin graft, punctured lung, beating throat. I was prepared for anything. The directions were framed and carried at all times. Each street spoke a different hum. We sat quietly waiting to be fed. We were only so many scraps, only so many holes to see through. My body was placed in a machine, pressed on. There was some comfort to that.

BEYOND THE CANVASSED SKY

After which the object gleamed clean and bright. What was there left to fear? The machines placed boxes on a conveyor belt, everything was measured down to the minute. The table was a place to bend the elbows, chairs were made of metal and skin. But, how does the mouth do that? How does it continue to move like a mindless pump?

GRIEF PRIMER

We learned many words would be lost: *books, mirrors, scarves and mittens, postcards, plays, pets, hot baths, sheet music, river stones polished to a pale red, picnics with lemon cake and coffee, early morning bird-calls, flashlights, photographs, record players, animals carved from birch trees, bicycles, movie theaters, red wine, crocheted blankets, carousels, houseplants and pianos...*

Each word we wrote on little slips of paper we hid under our tongues. *Our hearts became exiles, a silence settled in.*

NOW A FALSE WINDOW

What we knew was that our bodies held the illness in. Someone coughed, objects waited, our skin was more surface-wall than sense-organ, time was inescapable, nothing was expected of us except silence, the country we lived in had shut its door. We covered ourselves with what we had. We walked in circles and sometimes fell down. We had the day, the night. We had what we filled in our glasses. We found what could soothe our throats. Our bodies were not careless, we were. Thick drops escaped the stitching. We had all the reminders.

Disoriented digging, silence the tissue, silence the spotted life. Loudspeakers grew everywhere, tumors worn on sweaters.

TODAY'S LESSON

I dreamed I was walking in the woods with my dog. Pine trees towered over us scaffolding the sky in a sharp web of needles. Suddenly there was a dead owl, its body like a collapsed pillow in the snow. My dog sat next to the small body, stood guard as though the owl was only sleeping. All around us wind. Silence covered us like a heavy snowbank—

Through the night, through the forgotten room, the eyes a room, a locked away word.

WILD LIFE

The room was a caged field. We worried our neck skin, the scabs fragile and raised, a red bud pushed forth. The answers never heard. Our clothes were easily replaced, our wrists hung lifeless like collapsed boats. The plan was to be opened like a box. Pressed and straightened, our bodies contained all the stale pieces. Our lungs lost recognition. Everything was new. Everything still needed to be cleaned. We said, save that piece for later.

STUDYING THE PARTICLES
IN CLOUD MATTER

We noticed how each breath formed a structure. How that structure was a woven river against a steel-blue land. How the factory stood sharp and stark in an ochre sky. How smokestacks radiated ghost-shapes, a stale steward of production. How the mud-covered fields were dulled to bone after the first snow. How the snow spored the single tree's branches as though with mold. You have no security, the voice assured us. Those noises you hear each night are your own failing lungs.

The drawers filled quickly with our souvenirs of seashells and stones. A little body found on the ground meant nothing.

AVOIDANCE THEORY

I began to cover my arms with lists: *prepare your memory for observation, each morning greet the corners, open doors carefully, never lift your voice, never think of yesterday, never wish for warmth, eat what is given, hide any evidence, when the lungs begin to beat think of wind, when the mouth begins to fade think of sky, shut the window of your throat, fall asleep standing up, keep quiet, avoid the sun, avoid the stars, avoid contact of any kind, keep what is hidden, hidden.*

CROWD BEHAVIOR
DURING AN EMERGENCY

Grids of color streaked across the sky in a growth of green light. Colonies of automatons descended upon the land. We were clusters of pipes. We blindly stared, were people with the scrapings of hope. We cared about the dirt, the floors spanning out, the squares of cement. The voice spoke through the loudspeakers, it told us to leave. Our room was needed for another meeting. We shuffled our hands in the air. Something was burning but we shut the door. We did what we were told.

TRANSPLANT FACTORY

The animals outside were fox-like, they pawed away at the frozen ground in search of food. They lunged at the windows when they saw us moving inside the factory. Each morning I waited by my window to watch the animals begin their scavenging.

I noticed how the white walls were like the snow-covered field surrounding the factory. I asked the person next to me if she wanted my last piece of bread. She became nervous. She didn't know what to do with her arms hanging like heavy shovels.

TRANSPLANT FACTORY

The machines continued to move across the land like breathing oil rigs. Their digging wore down the frozen dirt to paper-thin piles. From the loudspeakers came a different voice. Tomorrow will begin a new system, the voice told us. You will decode the messages from the falling snow. Each person will wear her history on her skin. Make sure these parts of your skin remain exposed at all time.

Whatever was going to happen hadn't been named yet.

II.

TRANSPLANT FACTORY

Then the days passed and all we knew was work. We were a wordless mass leaning over like an immense frozen wave, lifting snow dull as dust. Someone wrote down our observations on a piece of paper: *the snow holds no shape, the wind controls everything, the sky is another pale blue canvas—*

We quickly tired. Our stomachs had become empty buckets inside our bodies. Soon our observations were labels of our desires. Then pleas. Then nothing.

PRODUCTIVITY PROPAGANDA

In the distance we saw a scrapyard of fallen things: broken machines piled with debris, a tangle of colorless trees, rust-covered engines, abandoned bicycles, bones and glass and dirty mattresses. We just scaled the surface. We believed our lips were on other people's faces. That what we had to say would arrive with neat edges, a clean shiny surface. Or, we would say nothing at all. We had questions. We were told scabs would cover our legs. The words were spoken through the loudspeakers and we were to trust that. We were to understand the appropriate sounds to make. But in our dreams our legs were fields of poppies.

A NEW ANIMAL

We didn't know what we were doing. We were trying to make the machines more human. Or, we were trying to make humans more like machines. Either way, the glass fell off the table. As usual, there was a silence in the back of the room, our throats like shelves, our hands empty containers waiting to be filled. Certainly it doesn't end this way. Each person braced for the next shock, and each shock reduced to an incident report.

THE MACHINES KNEW
TO BE CAREFUL THIS TIME

Our eyes offered us nothing, and in the end that was the reason we hid them in drawers. For later, for later. That was what we knew. Though our corners were still clean and neat, they told us the illness was now in the ground. We built signs about the division of land.

Eventually we sewed our lungs to our chests.

THE HEART BEGAN TO FORGET ITSELF

In our sleep the illness was disguised in a small patch of poppies. A blank face looked at me from the ceiling. Who doesn't love a doorway? *The night was disrupted, the night was a message never sent.* But the construction continued. The wind came to us at right angles. Behind the boxes were more boxes. *A pulsing happened there, a kept-organ.*

CONSIDERING THE PAPERWORK

Each day instructions were sent on the uses of the body.
Today we practiced bending our arms to embrace. Our
elbows were sharp windmills, our wrists were bolted joints.

A COLONY OF ANIMALS
WITHOUT EYES

We learned to sew our hands shut, to be very small, a thing forgotten. Even the stitching in our jackets reminded us. We knew something without knowing like an animal searching for a lost bone in a snowbank. I had a message to send through the wires. I said, I understand, I understand. Yes, the rooms meant something different now. Rows were made, places to rest our bodies at night.

ANATOMY OF DREAD

That was my heart, that beating piece, that thrown-over box.

If I had to believe in something. Whatever my throat was, kept-thing, caged-breath. Machines constantly moved like awkward metal animals, dug deep holes that punctured the dirt. Mostly I looked at objects. I lived like any other person in a room with a door and walls. I learned that all living things must be still to survive. I became a smokestack, a smothered statue, a slow and silent stalk.

THE MACHINE BODY

And though the wind whipped the piles of snow into a deadly undercurrent, though wires hung from low clouds like an electrical sea-stratus, though the sun was a dim and solitary shadow of itself, though the skin flattened, fell like ghost-ribbons, though the speaking part was hidden, a locked gate, a lonely handle, though memory was just a brief smudge of red, still—

ANOTHER THEORY

My mouth told me the field was broken. My mouth was a poppy, a thing that split in two. The river was straight and the landscape was a body stitched shut.

WE UNDERSTOOD CLARIFICATION
WAS NECESSARY

We had all the memory we could buy. We were able to see our lungs, how they caught themselves before departure. How communication was a form of wreckage. The machines felt sad, were things of land. And the messages were sent through an opened throat. The milk-sky held its position all day.

ANOTHER DEAD LANGUAGE

Then our hands withered, our eyes became cogs or the smallest pinecones on a single tall tree.

TRANSPLANT FACTORY

We noticed a pale apricot line of light at the horizon. We noticed wires no longer hung from the sky, clouds crowded near the ground like masses of smoke or coral. We wore our thick coats, watched the snow's endless screen of static. We had no idea how long we had been here. We huddled close together for warmth, waiting for the next set of instructions.

DURING SURVEILLANCE
SIDE EFFECTS MAY OCCUR

It was more a straining-change, a creased sky-mark, a flesh covered with picked scabs. Our bodies in rooms like boxes, our eyes like boxes without lids. Each conversation transcribed, our mouths connected to wires in the walls. Each movement a tremor, a record of our reaction. How could we hate our own organs? Were we changed people? Our hair fell to the ground. Everywhere we touched blood-red poppies surfaced.

We dreamed, we dreamed.

III.

TRANSPLANT FACTORY

We woke with a start. The loudspeakers roared awake, a deep pounding began. Your assignment today is to study the land's patterns. You will find slips of paper that contain instructions for forgetting the sun. Record your observations on your arms. Time has turned its back on you, the voice intoned.

All day endless instructions, words fell from the loudspeakers like thick strips of Morse code. No one cares how many breaths you take. Nothing waits for your return home. Your homes have disappeared like fallen airplanes in a forgotten sea.

HOMELAND SECURITY 1

I watched the sky turn to rotten tangerines. The fox-animals swept across the land in silent packs, a sea of red fur and teeth. Thin lines betrayed the land like lines betrayed the skin. A webbed-wound, an abandoned bird's nest. I swept the bone-floors clean. There was so much silence it was like walking away, then walking away again.

HOMELAND SECURITY 2

Be grateful for the shadow you saw yesterday. Be grateful for the walls, for the ceiling that doesn't snow, for the cold soup and stale husk of bread. Be grateful for the blindness of night, for your opaque sleep warm as pearled water. We were not safe here but couldn't leave.

O obvious violence, keep it to yourself.

BRIEF ENCOUNTER

A small catch. The mistake was recorded. Afterwards the
questions were bright mirrors thrown out the window.
Imagine a face cut off. How a person lived with her
hands sewn shut for years. Because the skin was also a flat
surface. It was still snowing. Lately the sky was dark all
day, the moon a deep cave. We shoved our hands into our
pockets. The air was something to touch.

WHEN THE SKY WAS
AN ABANDONED BUILDING

I picked over the scabbed fields as though they were my legs. I planted wires in the ground, rows of strange anemones. I dreamed of electric-yellow dahlias in my late summer garden, of my dog's speckled ears. I dreamed she was waiting for me just beyond the fence's boundary. Was there a way out? How did I begin to understand such a thing?

THE RITUALS OF SILENCE

O instruments of burden. O plastered bone-cages. We thought, this is only temporary. Or, the voice told us, this is only temporary. Did it matter? We knew the rules. If we wanted more the words were not there. Now the poppies were pulsing cups. The snow fell in swaths of dead skin cells.

MORNING CALISTHENICS

The voice drilled over the loudspeakers. Move your mouth. Smile. Now smile more. I closed my eyes and our faces became seagulls.

FROM THE WRECKAGE

We found the leftover living parts. They were small but didn't seem to notice. They had learned to unlock the door. Tomorrow they would go in search of food.

I told myself my hands were peppermint leaves I stuffed in my mouth.

A NEW HUNGER

Another violent sunset, suddenly thousands of seagulls swarmed the sky like an endless field of gray waves. The fading sunglow spread like wings, was molten and momentary. Was the instant just before nightfall. My heart opened and closed its mouth. The stale pieces were packed like feathers in my ribcage. And the too-bright tucked me into bed. *Look at the inside of my mouth, there, there was my soul, stupid wandering wretch groping around like an animal without eyes.*

PASSIVE RESISTENCE

We formed our own language. The different silences, how our mouths moved like moles above ground. Little scraps of paper meant hunger. Pieces of fabric in the corners meant warmth. A raised hand meant danger. Loneliness and desire were scratches along the walls, friendship a small tap on the window.

THE BODY GREW ANOTHER LAYER

What were we trying to escape now? My lungs knocked on the chest's door. Our messages were everywhere, scattered fingerprints smudged on windows. The voice told us, sit still, this world is meant to bind. Don't be difficult, your silence means nothing. *Pulse and pulsing. Fallen back intimacy. I've lost my human rendition.*

I was certain death pressed inside my stomach. The body became its own type of map. Dear little song under my wrist, that was how I loved.

POST TREATMENT

We thought we understood what was happening and then we found that we didn't. Our skin hung over the window stiff against the metal. Now the tugging and tying closed the hole of our bodies. It hurts, we told the machines. A small pocket of coral slept under our tongues. Our eyes weighed down our faces, our faces weighed down our bones, our bones became little clusters of regret.

I attempted companionship with the sink, then realized what I was doing. I undressed until only my bandage was showing and found myself in the window. What scar? I asked. What is exposed even after this?

HIBERNATION NOTES

We were here. We were here. We were here.

OF HOPE

But the dirty thread of yesterday pulled at our skin. Tomorrow we will tie our answers to the new wires hanging from the sky, tell the land we pray for it every night, tempt understanding with blindness, tempt blindness with heat, tempt heat with buckets of snow, tempt snow with sky, tempt sky with flight, tempt flight with a colony of shining clouds.

IV.

TRANSPLANT FACTORY

At night we started creating our own breathing maps. We searched the drawers for pencils and paper, each with her little compass of hope beating away. The land outside became large rectangles of reds, rows of black lines, woven nets of blue. We made the horizon a river of yellow rope. We turned the fences into bright flags. Our maps looked like relocated skin grafts or one big quilted plot.

FOR THE NEXT DISASTER

Our plan was to understand the variables: *if this paper grew an outer layer of skin, if this chest blinked its feeble eye, then*—When we felt the wall would we understand? In the roof of our mouths hung the breathing map. Lines circled back into themselves like bright orbiting atoms. We took the sky's position as warning. Just beneath, just beneath. We knew fire was necessary, a scar left over, a bowl full. Our makeshift hearts beat the same. The evening meant our mouths were a stunted rosebud, a sharp and senseless stone.

VIEW FROM THE BRIDGE

It was where nothing could touch us. Not the floor we sat on, not illness.

Dear dread, you are part of the steel beams, the stupid lit-up stars. *Here, take my line, my shaking lung. My cup needs more.*

TRANSPLANT FACTORY

And all the scratching of my heart. What horrible creature had crawled inside my chest? The maps were tucked away in the corners like diagramed snails slowly sliding around. *O effigies of escape.* I looked out the window to the fox-animals, their eyes flickering in the dark moon-shadows. The snow was a ground-ghost. I leaned against the person next to me. Even this small contact made me weep.

TRANSPLANT FACTORY

We hadn't heard new instructions for days. One morning there was no bread left for us outside. We huddled together, whispered, touched our faces to make sure we were still alive. We unrolled the maps, memorized the star-patterns, studied the lines between land and sky, horizon and sea. Outside I saw a shadow run away. Outside the fields became frozen hurricane-waves. At night we slept in tight rows like a heaving crop so close our arms touched.

BEFORE THE LAST SNOW

The sun was just beginning to fade away to a dirty violet. We wandered the fields searching for any leftovers we could find: half-formed onions, frozen tomatoes filled with rotten spots, sprouted potatoes, corn husks. I said pilfer this, pilfer that. We must steal all we can. I can admit this now, my face was a trapdoor.

BEYOND THE BOARDED SKY

The ground shook, wires fell from the sky in a single snarl of dark seaweed. The returning happened with paper and fire, with wave and wind. The sky was given then taken away. Even the single tree was uprooting itself to find a new home.

SURVIVAL GUIDE

The future became a sea exploding to red. The rugs pulled themselves away when we walked through the room. We had learned to sit with our little mouths like opened cans. A fluorescent bulb fell from the ceiling, glass shattered into sharp piles of frozen-brightness. Our lungs dislocated themselves. We walked up and down the halls and waited for the coral foam of light again.

TRANSPLANT FACTORY

Finally we decided it was time. We opened the door. The morning offered itself to us clean and bright, the sky a field of poppies. Frozen automatons scattered the land in a mountain of metal bodies. Everything was fenced off. The horizon's quartered corners, the frozen crop's constellation of fallen vines. In the distance a single electrical tower stood like a six-armed totem.

TRANSPLANT FACTORY

Our necks became maps, our bodies their own countries. What was waiting for us in the distance? Who would forgive this?

We left the door open and walked away. No, we left the door open and never again returned.

ABOUT THE AUTHOR

Carrie Bennett is a Massachusetts Cultural Council Artist Fellow and author of *biography of water* (The Word Works, 2005, winner of the Washington Prize) as well as chapbooks from Dancing Girl Press: *The Quiet Winter* (2012), *Animals in Pretty Cages* (2013), and *The Affair Fragments* (2015). Her poetic project, *Expedition Notes*, was published as an ephemerabook by Letter [r] Press (2014). She holds an MFA in poetry from the Iowa Writers' Workshop where she was a Maytag Fellow. Bennett teaches writing at Boston University and lives in Somerville, Massachusetts, with her family.

ABOUT THE ARTIST

Cheri Jacobs is an interior designer and artist based in Phoenix, Arizona.

ABOUT THE WORD WORKS

The Word Works, a nonprofit literary organization, publishes contemporary poetry and presents public programs. The Hilary Tham Capital Collection presents work by poets who volunteer for literary nonprofit organizations. Nomination forms are requested from qualifying nonprofits by April 15 and manuscript submissions from nominated poets by May 1. Other imprints include the Washington Prize, International Editions, and The Tenth Gate Prize. A reading period is also held in May.

Monthly, The Word Works offers free literary programs in the Chevy Chase, MD, Café Muse series, and each summer, it holds free poetry programs in Washington, D.C.'s Rock Creek Park. Annually in June, two high school students debut in the Joaquin Miller Poetry Series as winners of the Jacklyn Potter Young Poets Competition. Since 1974, Word Works programs have included: "In the Shadow of the Capitol," a symposium and archival project on the African American intellectual community in segregated Washington, D.C.; the Gunston Arts Center Poetry Series; the Poet Editor panel discussions at The Writer's Center; and Master Class workshops.

As a 501(c)3 organization, The Word Works has received awards from the National Endowment for the Arts, the National Endowment for the Humanities, the D.C. Commission on the Arts & Humanities, the Witter Bynner Foundation, Poets & Writers, The Writer's Center, Bell Atlantic, the David G. Taft Foundation, and others, including many generous private patrons.

The Word Works has established an archive of artistic and administrative materials in the Washington Writing Archive housed in the George Washington University Gelman Library. It is a member of the Council of Literary Magazines and Presses and its books are distributed by Small Press Distribution.

wordworksbooks.org

THE HILARY THAM CAPITAL COLLECTION

Mel Belin, *Flesh That Was Chrysalis*

Doris Brody, *Judging the Distance*

Sarah Browning, *Whiskey in the Garden of Eden*

Grace Cavalieri, *Pinecrest Rest Haven*

Cheryl Clarke, *By My Precise Haircut*

Christopher Conlon, *Gilbert and Garbo in Love*
            & *Mary Falls: Requiem for Mrs. Surratt*

Donna Denizé, *Broken like Job*

W. Perry Epes, *Nothing Happened*

Bernadette Geyer, *The Scabbard of Her Throat*

Barbara G. S. Hagerty, *Twinzilla*

James Hopkins, *Eight Pale Women*

Brandon Johnson, *Love's Skin*

Marilyn McCabe, *Perpetual Motion*

Judith McCombs, *The Habit of Fire*

James McEwen, *Snake Country*

Miles David Moore, *The Bears of Paris*
            & *Rollercoaster*

Kathi Morrison-Taylor, *By the Nest*

Tera Vale Ragan, *Reading the Ground*

Michael Shaffner, *The Good Opinion of Squirrels*

Maria Terrone, *The Bodies We Were Loaned*

Hilary Tham, *Bad Names for Women*
            & *Counting*

Barbara Louise Ungar, *Charlotte Brontë, You Ruined My Life*
            & *Immortal Medusa*

Jonathan Vaile, *Blue Cowboy*

Rosemary Winslow, *Green Bodies*

Michele Wolf, *Immersion*

Joe Zealberg, *Covalence*

THE TENTH GATE PRIZE

Jennifer Barber, *Works on Paper*, 2015
Lisa Sewell, *Impossible Object*, 2014

THE WASHINGTON PRIZE

Nathalie F. Anderson, *Following Fred Astaire*, 1998
Michael Atkinson, *One Hundred Children Waiting for a Train*, 2001
Molly Bashaw, *The Whole Field Still Moving Inside It*, 2013
Carrie Bennett, *biography of water*, 2004
Peter Blair, *Last Heat*, 1999
John Bradley, *Love-in-Idleness: The Poetry of Roberto Zingarello*,
        1995, 2nd edition 2014
Christopher Bursk, *The Way Water Rubs Stone*, 1988
Richard Carr, *Ace*, 2008
Jamison Crabtree, *Rel[AM]ent*, 2014
Barbara Duffey, *Simple Machines*, 2015
B. K. Fischer, *St. Rage's Vault*, 2012
Linda Lee Harper, *Toward Desire*, 1995
Ann Rae Jonas, *A Diamond Is Hard but Not Tough*, 1997
Frannie Lindsay, *Mayweed*, 2009
Richard Lyons, *Fleur Carnivore*, 2005
Elaine Magarrell, Blameless Lives, 1991
Fred Marchant, *Tipping Point*, 1993, 2nd edition 2013
Ron Mohring, *Survivable World*, 2003
Barbara Moore, *Farewell to the Body*, 1990
Brad Richard, *Motion Studies*, 2010
Jay Rogoff, *The Cutoff*, 1994
Prartho Sereno, *Call from Paris*, 2007, 2nd edition 2013
Enid Shomer, *Stalking the Florida Panther*, 1987
John Surowiecki, *The Hat City After Men Stopped Wearing Hats*, 2006
Miles Waggener, *Phoenix Suites*, 2002
Charlotte Warren, *Gandhi's Lap*, 2000
Mike White, *How to Make a Bird with Two Hands*, 2011
Nancy White, *Sun, Moon, Salt*, 1992, 2nd edition 2010
George Young, *Spinoza's Mouse*, 1996

INTERNATIONAL EDITIONS

Kajal Ahmad (Alana Marie Levinson-LaBrosse, Mewan
      Nahro Said Sofi, and Darya Abdul-Karim Najin, trans.,
      with Barbara Goldberg), *Handful of Salt*
Keyne Cheshire (trans.), *Murder at Jagged Rock: A Tragedy*
      by Sophocles
Yoko Danno & James C. Hopkins, *The Blue Door*
Moshe Dor, Barbara Goldberg, Giora Leshem, eds., *The Stones*
      Remember: Native Israeli Poets
Moshe Dor (Barbara Goldberg, trans.), *Scorched by the Sun*
Lee Sang (Myong-Hee Kim, trans.), *Crow's Eye View:*
      The Infamy of Lee Sang, Korean Poet
Vladimir Levchev (Henry Taylor, trans.), *Black Book of the*
      Endangered Species

ADDITIONAL TITLES

Karren L. Alenier, *Wandering on the Outside*
Karren L. Alenier & Miles David Moore, eds.,
      Winners: A Retrospective of the Washington Prize
Karren L. Alenier, ed., *Whose Woods These Are*
Christopher Bursk, ed., *Cool Fire*
Grace Cavalieri, *Creature Comforts*
Barbara Goldberg, *Berta Broadfoot and Pepin the Short*
Frannie Lindsay, *If Mercy*
Marilyn McCabe, *Glass Factory*
W.T. Pfefferle, *My Coolest Shirt*
Ayaz Pirani, *Happy You Are Here*
Jacklyn Potter, Dwaine Rieves, Gary Stein, eds.,
      Cabin Fever: Poets at Joaquin Miller's Cabin
Robert Sargent, *Aspects of a Southern Story*
      & *A Woman from Memphis*
Nancy White, ed., *Word for Word*

CPSIA information can be obtained
at www.ICGtesting.com
Printed in the USA
FFOW05n2231100316

9 781944 585006